# Life's Lessons

**Insights & Information
for a Richer Life!**

Rebecca L. Morgan, CSP, CMC

*Life's Lessons: Insights and Information for a Richer Life*

© 2009 All rights reserved. No part of this book may be reproduced or transmitted in any form or by any means, electronic or mechanical, including photocopying, recording, or by any information storage or retrieval system, without the written permission from the copyright holder, except for the inclusion of quotations in a review.

Printed in the United States of America.

ISBN eBook: 978-0-9660740-2-4

printed book: 978-0-9660740-1-7

How to order:

Quantity copies may be ordered directly from www.RebeccaMorgan.com.

Visit us online for updates and additional articles.

*Life's Lessons*

This book is dedicated to you — someone interested in being the best you can possibly be.

!!!

# Books by Rebecca Morgan

## Books

- Calming Upset Customers
- Grow Your Key Talent: Thought-Provoking Essays for Business Owners, Executives and Managers on Developing Star Staff
- Inspiring Others to Win
- Life's Lessons: Insights and Information for a Richer Life
- Professional Selling: Practical Secrets for Successful Sales
- Remarkable Customer Service ... and Disservice: Case Studies and Discussions to Increase Your Customers' Delight
- TurboTime: Maximizing Your Results Through Technology

## MP3s

- Making Time Work For You
- Recipe for Customer Service Success

All can be ordered at www.RebeccaMorgan.com

# Contents

| | |
|---|---|
| Introduction | vii |
| About the Author | ix |
| A Formula For Growth | 1 |
| Components of Mastery | 5 |
| Being Coached To Be Your Best | 9 |
| Life's Lessons | 13 |
| Giving Yourself a Motivational Talk | 17 |
| Giving Verbal Hugs | 19 |
| Creating Your Own Paradise | 21 |
| Giving up Good for Better | 23 |
| Waves Are Like People | 25 |
| What's In A Name? | 27 |
| Taking Calculated Risks | 29 |
| Even Communication Experts Miscommunicate | 35 |
| The Power of Commitment | 37 |
| Frivolous Talk | 43 |
| Are You Listening? | 45 |
| The Trail As Life | 49 |
| Leadership Walk | 53 |

| | |
|---|---|
| Borrowing Courage | 57 |
| Lessons From a Horse | 61 |
| Taking a Stand | 65 |
| Trust Your Guides | 69 |
| Hard-Won Lessons | 73 |
| Being a Conscious Conversationalist | 77 |
| The Power of Our Words | 82 |
| Resources | 99 |

# Introduction

This book is for anyone interested in improving their lives. It's full of my personal experiences, observations and lessons. There's not a lot of how-to, but more insights from my life.

## How to use this book

- ***See how my lessons parallel those from your own life:*** Have you learned similar lessons or different ones? Do my insights add to those you've already learned?

- ***Learn from "OPE" — Other People's Experiences:*** If one is astute, you learn from your own life experiences. Some of these are positive — some are negative. It is less painful to learn from other people's unpleasant experiences!

- ***Share with others:*** Read these stories at your staff meeting or family dinner table and discuss the lessons. Facilitate a discussion to adapt the lessons to each person's life.

*Life's Lessons*

I welcome your sharing your ideas, suggestions, and your stories for future volumes.

*Life's Lessons*

# About the Author

Rebecca Morgan is an internationally recognized consultant, trainer, facilitator and speaker, based in San José, CA.

Rebecca partners with clients to create innovative, long-lasting professional development solutions. Her focus is strategic customer service, and increasing people-productivity by providing the right skills for the right people in the right way.

Many recognizable organizations have engaged Rebecca to develop creative solutions to their situations. These include: Apple Computer, Singapore Airlines, Wells Fargo Bank, New York Life Insurance, Microsoft, ING, Hewlett-Packard, Adobe, Applied Materials, Quantum, Seagate, Sun Microsystems, Lockheed Martin, Sony, and Stanford University, among many, many more.

Rebecca is one of America's most respected and sought-after customer service experts, professional development consultants, authors and speakers.

Her media appearances include 60 Minutes, The Oprah Winfrey Show, National Public Radio's Market Place, *USA Today*, *Wall Street Journal*, *San José Mercury News*, Malaysia's *Star* newspaper, Singapore's *Straight Times*, *the Brunei Times* and the San Francisco Chronicle. Her ideas are so solid, last year Microsoft hired her as their workplace effectiveness spokesperson.

Rebecca's books, recordings, videos and learning tools exemplify the excellence she creates in all of her work. She's authored four popular books — two have been translated into nine languages. Additionally, she's coauthored four others; one is a fund-raiser for the US Olympic team. Her books include: *Calming Upset Customers*, *Remarkable Customer Service...And Disservice*, *Grow Your Key Talent*, *TurboTime: Maximizing Your Results Through Technology*, *Professional Selling: Practical Secrets for Successful Sales*, and *Life's Lessons: Insights and Information for a Richer Life*.

## *One of an Elite Few Professionals*

Rebecca is committed to continuous learning and growing, especially since that is what she imparts to others. She has demonstrated this striving by receiving the Certified Speaking Professional (CSP) designation conferred by the National Speakers Association (NSA). At the time, the ten-year-old designation had been earned by only 215 people in the world—less than seven percent of the 3700 members of NSA.

The CSP is a designation of achievement earned through proven speaking experience. It is awarded to individuals who have completed a comprehensive application process and met NSA's stringent criteria.

She has also earned the professional designation Certified Management Consultant (CMC) from the Institute of Management Consultants (IMC). She is the fifteenth professional in the world to earn both the CSP and the CMC designations.

Candidates for the CMC undergo a thorough investigation of their consulting experience. They are interviewed by a panel of senior consultants to verify their competence. Additionally, candidates must pass a written examination demonstrating their knowledge of the IMC's Code of Ethics.

*Awareness is a process, rather than a goal*

# A Formula For Growth

*"Why stay we on the earth except to grow?"*

—Robert Browning

Most people would agree with Browning. Unfortunately, growth doesn't always come easily; often we feel "stuck." If you're feeling stuck, here's a formula to help you get unstuck:

## Awareness

Awareness is the knowledge of our strengths, weaknesses, goals, and desires. As we become aware, the picture becomes clear. Vaguely amorphous feelings become focused and gain power, much as a ray of morning light broadens into day..

We increase awareness through introspection, creativity, classes and workshops, counseling, reading, and honest talks with friends, family, co-workers, even bosses. Awareness is a process, rather than a goal.

The force of awareness carries its own motivation. For example, a smoker who experiences severe chest pains (awareness) may quit smoking with surprising ease.

If the stakes are high enough, we translate awareness into action, e.g., growth, without much discipline.

More often than not, however, the immediate stakes are not so high, so obvious or so tangible that awareness creates action. More often, we see the wisdom of changing our behavior while we continue our old patterns.

## + Self-Discipline

To break out of old patterns we need discipline. Athletes have coaches and musicians have teachers to provide both awareness and discipline. Most of the time, though, you're on your own.

How can you be your own coach? Begin by focusing on your goal, visualizing the outcome, and creating a plan (e.g., start with manageable steps, write them down, and keep promises made to yourself). You might enlist a friend as a surrogate coach to help you stay on track.

But sometimes nothing seems to work. No matter what you do, you remain stuck in old patterns. How do you know when to give up? When the effort is not worth the payoff? When your progress isn't commensurate with the time you spend? Or maybe you never give up.

## = Growth

We don't achieve every goal we set for ourselves, but we can grow from every attempt we make—no matter what the outcome. For this reason our formula does not equal "success" or "results." We won't always succeed. However, if we choose, we can grow to a new level of wisdom.

So the formula itself isn't magic. It is, however, a shorthand method to help us remember why we put ourselves through painful and difficult situations, and why we deny ourselves certain pleasures. We like the feeling of working through the equation. We like the feeling of growth. We like knowing that we are better than we were before.

*Even top pros continue to work to become better*

*Life's Lessons*

# *Components of Mastery*

Often, people attend my presentations looking for new ideas. Sometimes they know what to do, and they're looking for the motivation to do it. This got me thinking about mastery. As a result, I've developed a five-step formula for mastery.*

Sometimes we're seeking ways to become better at our jobs. Or we want to learn how to have a more fulfilling relationship with someone we care about, manage our time better, close sales more successfully, or lead a more healthy life style. Although you may be good at many things in your life, would you consider yourself a master at them? Even top pros continue to work to become better.

It impresses me while watching the Olympics, to realize that these athletes, many of whom hold world records, still see room for improvement. They all have coaches, they all practice untold hours, they all strive for their own personal best.

Why, a number of years ago, did Bonnie Blair go for her fifth gold medal when she already had four? I think it was because she knew she could do better. She not only got the fifth gold, but she set a new world record.

In order to pursue and practice mastery, follow these five steps:

## 1. Desire change.

- You must believe something must change.
- You must believe you must change it.
- You must believe you can change it.

## 2. Explore your attitude about the results of the change.

Explore both positive and negative results. How will your life be different? What are your fears about the change? What are the benefits it will bring? What will it cost you?

## 3. Know the process to institute the new behavior.

Just wishing for change is not very effective. When you want to master a new skill, you need to know how to acquire that skill or behavior. How can you learn about mastery in this area? Read a book? Attend a seminar? Enlist a mentor? Get a coach?

## 4. Use the new behavior regularly.

Practice. Just like Bonnie Blair. Practice does not make perfect. It makes permanent. You could be cementing poor habits. Only perfect practice makes perfect. Few people ever achieve perfection in any endeavor. However, an overriding concern for perfection can mentally paralyze us and make us not practice.

## 5. Enjoy the benefits of change, no matter how small.

How does it feel when you have glimpses of a higher level of mastery? When you're in the "zone"—even if it's leading an effective business meeting, giving a heartfelt talk, or telling someone you love them—it feels great! Relish that feeling. It will keep you going if you trip and fall on your road to mastery.

*I'm sure some of this is from seminars I've attended, books and articles I've read, and conversations I've had with people over the last thirty years. I don't have anyone specific to whom I can attribute any of this to. It's an amalgamation of many sources, none of which I can identify.*

*Life's Lessons*

**We have mastered certain skills in our work and life, but there are still areas in which we know we're not competent**

# Being Coached To Be Your Best

When was the last time you had a coach? In high school or college sports? When you were beginning your career? Maybe never?

I've worked with several coaches. At first I found the relationship difficult. They would tell me to do something that I didn't want to do or was difficult. I argued that their ideas wouldn't work. I wouldn't be able to do it. I'd fail. Then I'd beat myself up.

Finally, with my health and fitness coach, June Anderson, owner of Fitness For Success, I realized that my way hadn't worked, so why was I arguing with her? After all, I'd hired her to help me accomplish what I hadn't been able to achieve on my own. Although I knew what to do, I wasn't doing what I knew consistently enough to produce the results I wanted.

As adults we have mastered certain skills in our work and life, but there are still areas in which we know we're not competent. It was difficult, yet helpful, to think of myself as a beginner in areas in which I didn't yet have mastery. For example, June told me to drink six to eight glasses of water a day. I had been drinking zero glasses a day. When I drank four glasses I felt bloated and water logged. I tried to convince her that six to eight were too many. She didn't listen. We started with two as my goal, then when I was drinking two, we moved to three, then four. I still don't drink eight glasses every day, but I'm a lot closer than I was.

June knew when to ignore my protests. Gently yet firmly she urged me along with what seemed like simple to apply suggestions, yet they were hard for me to actually do. She saw my capabilities beyond what I saw.

I was rarely exercising more than once a week. My goal in the beginning was to exercise three times a week. I didn't see how I could do it. I hated exercise. I was busy traveling. I was busy fulfilling projects for clients. Now I exercise much more than before. She coached me to go beyond what I thought was possible.

I felt embarrassed that I needed a coach to help me do things I already knew I should be doing. "After all," my ego reasoned, "I'm a professional who runs a successful company, has written several books, and is in demand around the country. Why should I need a coach to get me to drink eight glasses of water? How ridiculous. I should be able to do this on my own."

The parallel to my own work struck me. In my presentations I remind people to do what they already know to do, but they aren't doing it. My audience members are intelligent, accomplished individuals who aren't doing what they know to do. I realized that I help them make commitments to follow through, to act upon the ideas we discuss.

Now I embrace the chance to be coached. I know that even Joe Montana and Steve Young had throwing coaches, and Jerry Rice, a catching coach. They didn't say, "Hey, I'm at the top of my game. I don't need anyone to tell me how to do what I do best." Their attitude is "Help me get just a few more yards out of a throw," or "Help me leap higher to catch this one."

It's not easy, but I think coaching is essential to being your best. Be willing to be a beginner toward mastery.

*Learning can happen, even if the lessons come from watching your own arrogance, stubbornness, and pain.*

# Life's Lessons

I helped behind the scenes at a powerful nine-day personal growth intensive program that I'd attended as a participant a year before. I'd not assisted at this program before so I was feeling new to everything.

As a participant, I'd felt that all my needs were cared for, and I never noticed the behind-the-scenes activity that made the program run so smoothly. Now, I was one of the dozens making it happen.

As an assistant, I had almost as many insights as when I was a participant. When the situation is right, learning can happen, even if the lessons come from watching your own arrogance, stubbornness, and pain.

I share my learning in the hope that it may help you avoid some of my lessons learned the hard way.

## 1. Be a "yes"

When your focus is truly to serve, it doesn't matter what job you're assigned to do. Say "yes" to each job with willingness and enthusiasm, no matter how mundane or distasteful it seems. I watched one man who was assigned the job of cleaning bathrooms every day. He accepted with a smile and positivity I'm afraid I couldn't have mustered. I learned to say "yes" with a smile, even if I wasn't feeling so positive at first. Then I found a way to turn the task into a gift.

For example, my first day, I was in charge of filling water glasses for the 50 volunteers. This assignment seemed mundane and tedious, but I remembered the lesson. I turned the task into a gift. As I filled each glass, I wished this water would help the volunteer focus on helping the participants with their breakthroughs.

The next day one of my duties was to type into the computer some messages written by the participants. At first I felt that this job was too lowly for me—after all, do they know who I am? But my indignation fell away when I learned that I was chosen because I was the most advanced Macintosh user there, and these messages were very important. In fact, as I learned later, it was an honor to read the private messages that were sent to the program's facilitator.

Do you ever have to do jobs that you don't want to do? Scrubbing floors, cleaning garages, filing, writing reports? Of course, we all have to do things we don't want to do. See if there's a way to say "yes" to the task, and do it as if it were a gift.

## 2. Don't let others' assessments sway you.

On my first day I was assigned to a team leader who was to show me my tasks. Earlier, she commented to me about several others on the team. "I know you can handle this task, but Maureen and Wendy can't even fill the water glasses right. They seem to be unable to do even the simplest tasks correctly."

I found myself responding to Maureen and Wendy similarly. I'd already made an assessment that they were incompetent at most everything. I began discounting them. If I needed advice on a job, I ignored them.

The next day I learned that they had assisted many times, even more than my team leader. They were very competent in the running of the program. I was dismayed by how easily I'd allowed myself to be swayed by someone else's assessment. I hadn't given Maureen and Wendy a chance to show me how much they knew.

### 3. *Be willing to be incompetent.*

The following day I was to write down the participants' names as they shared about their breakthroughs.

At first it was an easy task as one or two would stand at a time, with some time in between, as others prepared themselves to share. Then the pace quickened with four or five in quick succession.

The pace kept up, and I got behind. I missed some of the names. The man I reported to pointed this out, although I already knew it. What I had remembered as a jubilant time as a participant, turned into a nightmare for me as a volunteer. I was near tears.

The next day, after sharing my frustration with a few fellow volunteers, they helped me see that part of my frustration was from feeling incompetent. I was in a foreign situation, asked to do things precisely, and then messed up a seemingly simple task.

I realized that I don't often allow myself to be incompetent—a beginner, if that sounds better to you. Although I try new things, they're built upon actions in which I've been successful.

I vowed to be incompetent—a beginner—more often, to learn and experience things outside my base of competency. Then I won't be so rattled when I'm faced with experiences far from my comfort zone.

Are you willing to be a beginner? Are you willing to not do well at something that seems simple? Are you willing to learn from the experience, not just how to do the job better, but how to be gracious even when messing up something important? I know I have a long way to go to become a master in this area.

*Life's Lessons*

# Giving Yourself a Motivational Talk

Have you had those days when you were really stressed, things weren't going right, and finally that one last thing happened and you snapped? You yelled at someone you shouldn't have, or reacted differently than you would have liked?

A few years ago I had such an outburst. I was helping to run a conference for 600 professional colleagues. Even with months of pre-planning, there were glitches. The final straw happened on the second of three days. Something major had been missed, something I felt was someone else's responsibility that I now had to fix, because Carolyn had dropped the ball. Again.

Fixing this would mean a lot of work. I did it, but I was angry about it. The anger built until I saw Terry, the chair for the event. He had nothing to do with this glitch, but I ranted and raved about what was wrong and how I had to fix it. He got caught up in my emotional torrent, and he thought the sky had fallen. He rushed away to see for himself.

After seeing his reaction, I realized that I hadn't

handled the situation well. I'd created more upset than necessary because I was angry with Carolyn. I knew I had to change my attitude, or I'd allow other things to send me over the edge. After all, we had another day-and-a-half to go.

I found a quiet place and gave myself a motivational talk. You know—the talk a coach, mentor, or advisor would give you. "It's not the end of the world. Glitches happen. A pro handles them with grace. Lighten up and enjoy the conference. When the next glitch happens, just handle it with ease, don't even bother to tell Terry about it. He has many other things on his mind. That's why he put you in charge of this, because he knows things will be handled."

It helped. I entered the afternoon events with a "can do" attitude. I apologized to Terry for bothering him with the glitch. The rest of the conference went much better. Even though there were other problems, I handled them with a better attitude.

How can you give yourself a motivational talk the next time a glitch happens? What would you say? It may be helpful to prepare the threads of this talk beforehand. You never know when you might need a good talking to!

# Giving Verbal Hugs

These days we have to be so careful about touching people, yet we still want to embrace others, to show them we're glad to see them, that we care about them.

Try a verbal hug instead.

A verbal hug is a sincere acknowledgment, said to make the person feel warm, loved, and honored. For example, instead of greeting someone with the trite "How are you?" try "It's so good to see you," or, if it's true, "You're looking great."

When ending a telephone conversation, instead of "See you later," try "It was really good to talk to you," or "It was great to catch up with you," or "I'm glad things are going well for you."

Make a point to tell the person one thing you admire about them, "You know, I've always admired how you have such patience with challenging people." Or reinforce a success with "You worked hard. You deserve it."

Also, try a verbal massage—it's powerful. Have a group of friends, family or associates spend one minute sharing positive characteristics about one of your group. Then go on to the next person for one minute. Everyone calls out their sincere thoughts about each person. Comments like "nice shirt," or "you're not as obnoxious as you used to be," aren't what we're looking for here.

I call it a verbal massage because when it's your turn to be the recipient, you'll feel so great, it's like just coming out of a revitalizing massage.

So, who can you "hug" today?

*Life's Lessons*

# Creating Your Own Paradise

Do you sometimes feel that all you do is chores? You do chores at work (meetings, incessant calls, constant interruptions, boring paperwork) and at home (laundry, cooking, paying bills, picking up around the house, fixing things, running the kids to their activities). When do you have time for fun? When was the last time you did something that you really wanted to do?

I realized how prevalent this lifestyle was when I was conducting a workshop in Hawaii. We were discussing building time into our lives to enjoy where we lived. I asked them when was the last time that they went to the beach, hiked in the forest, or enjoyed the paradise around them. They said, "We're too busy doing laundry, cleaning house, working, and taking care of the kids. It isn't always paradise to those of us who live here."

I was surprised. Then I realized that I, too, live in a paradise, the San Francisco Bay Area, and yet I hadn't experienced much of the richness available to me. I discussed this with Robert. Living in an entrepreneurial household, we work long hours and long days. There's always a new project to work on—an article, newsletter, tape, presentation, or promotional package. We weren't allowing much time to recharge our batteries and enjoy our own paradise.

A few weeks later, Robert asked what I'd like for my upcoming birthday. I said, "I don't want more 'stuff.' I have enough stuff. I'd like an experience." That birthday he gave me the promise of an outing a month, of my choosing. Each month we would do something that I thought would be interesting.

One month we kayaked in a slough in Monterey Bay. Another, we hiked and picnicked with friends. We strolled through a Japanese tea garden for a morning. Once we took in a comedy show with friends in San Francisco then stayed overnight in the city. We stayed in a Santa Cruz inn with a private hot tub on a cliff overlooking the ocean. We hiked in a regional park 15 minutes away from our home. We bicycled to a local crafts fair. We took in a matinee of one of our favorite performers, along with lunch with friends.

Although I've lived in the Bay Area since 1966, there are many things I've never seen or done. Each month is a mini-adventure, and we're discovering things about our area we've never seen before.

Robert has given me a most precious gift—the gift of time and sweet memories.

*Life's Lessons*

# *Giving up Good for Better*

*"If it ain't broke, don't fix it."*

*"It works for me, so why should I change?"*

*"Better is the enemy of good."*

Y ou've got this great opening for your presentation. It works every time. It always gets a laugh. Why should you mess with a sure thing?

But maybe only half of your audience laughs. "Yes, but that half laughs loudly," you say. "It works. It's good."

Sure it's good, but is it the best you can do? Could you create an opening that would make 3/4 of the audience laugh? Can you create a funnier, more powerful, more poignant, more original opening? Probably. But to do that we have to be willing to give up good in order to be better.

I have an opening story that's good. It's unique to me, it's funny, it sets the tone. But women laugh more than men do. Do I use that story every time? No. Hardly ever anymore. Only with predominantly female audiences. "Why give it up?" you ask. "It works."

Because I knew I could do better.

Is giving up good easy? No. Half an audience laughing loudly is satisfying to us. The hardest part of giving up good is recognizing that it's only good, and that we can do better. Then we must play and tweak, or begin all over again, until we replace it with better.

Working to improve is the sign of a true professional. When we become satisfied with good, we become stagnant and lose our freshness, creativity, and zest. We're just going through the motions. The professionals in all vocations whom I most admire are those who are continually mastering their craft. Does a surgeon stop attending conferences or reading medical journals because her appendectomies are good? Not if she wants to get better. Does a top chef stop experimenting and trying new recipes? Never!

What do you need to give up that's good in order to make it even better?

*Life's Lessons*

# *Waves Are Like People*

The morning was spectacular—a warm Gulf breeze brushed my cheeks. Waves scampered across the beach.

Meditating on the waves' delicious sound, color and dance, I observed that even as they were approaching the shore, they were retreating.

A small berm lay between me and the surf. A few waves crossed the crest and scurried toward me. But most were spent before reaching the top.

I tried to discern which wave would make it over the top. At first, I thought I could tell by the size of the swell. Surely the largest would make it over. No.

Turning when I heard a loud crash, I thought, "That one will surely make it over." No.

Then it hit me. These waves are like people. And the metaphor machine kicked into motion.

- Even as people move forward, progress is pitted with forces pulling us back. Sometimes we give into these forces when the pressure is too great. Sometimes we still progress despite the resistance.

- We never know what power is inside people that propels them over the top. It's invisible. Sometimes these people aren't even aware that it's there.

- People who come on the loudest, often don't have what it takes to ascend the crest.

- People who look like they have the power to make it, often don't. They may look like winners on the outside, but they are missing the power inside to succeed.

- Achievers are often quiet in their pursuits. We wouldn't necessarily predict that they were going to make it.

*Life's Lessons*

# What's In A Name?

My friend and I are at Charles and Suzanne's cocktail party. We sit next to someone we don't know.

I introduce myself, "Hello. I'm Rebecca." Shaking my hand, the stranger replies, "Hi, Becky. I'm Bill Hawkins."

"Hi, Bill," my friend offers his hand, "I'm Robert."

"Good to meet you, Bob. How do you know Susie and Chuck?"

Already Robert and I know a lot about Bill. We know that he doesn't listen, or he doesn't care about getting our names right, or that he's trying to be too familiar. And we don't like it.

Right or wrong, we make assumptions about Bill based on this one behavior. Later, if he suggests a business deal, we would already be on guard. Bill starts out with two strikes against him.

When people introduce themselves, the name they give is how they want to be addressed. If we had wanted to be called "Becky" and "Bob," that's how we would have introduced ourselves.

One of our friends has high visibility in our professional organization. She introduces herself as "Patricia," yet some who want to demonstrate their chuminess with her call her "Pat" or "Patty." This immediately signals to those of us who do know her that the offenders don't. They try to seem closer to Patricia than they really are.

Even worse is when someone who introduces you as a "good friend" mispronounces your name or gives the wrong name. It is embarrassing to correct the introducer; but you need to do so, otherwise the new person will call you by the wrong name. You could politely say to the introducer, "I'm sorry, I guess I haven't told you, I go by Rebecca instead of Becky."

If you find yourself with someone whose name is Richard, ask him what he prefers to be called. Don't assume that he is a "Dick," "Rick," or "Rich" without verifying it. Robert could also be a Rob. Suzanne could be Sue or Suzy. And, Suzanne and Susan are not the same.

Dale Carnegie said, "A person's name is to him or her the sweetest and most important sound in any language." Take responsibility to listen and use the right name.

*Life's Lessons*

# Taking Calculated Risks

*"Take calculated risks. That is quite different from being rash." —George S. Patton from a letter to Cadet George S. Patton IV, June 6, 1944*

Taking calculated risks means boldness with forethought. It means weighing the outcome and avoiding unwise action. A calculated risk might be giving a presentation to your boss' peers, telling someone they have a habit that annoys you, volunteering for a project you've never done before, or trying a new sport.

We can learn to take calculated risks, and they get easier with repeated attempts. Eventually you learn that you can pick yourself up and continue even if your boldness causes you to fall flat.

Morgan W. McCall Jr., coauthor of *What It Takes: Decision Makers at Work* conducted a study comparing 20 successful Fortune 500 executives with 20 whose careers hadn't been successful. One difference he found was that the achievers were secure enough to admit their fallibility, and they handled their mistakes with poise and grace. They analyzed their mistakes and learned from them, but they didn't become obsessed. "Executive achievers don't dwell on their mistakes and aren't afraid to take risks for fear of failing again," says McCall.

Many times it has been difficult for me to overcome my initial paralysis when faced with a risky challenge. Years ago when I entered the pension business, my boss assigned me to call on one tax attorney per day. Attorneys intimidated me. I almost had a heart attack.

My comfort zone was narrow. I felt comfortable calling on other insurance agents to ask them to recommend our services, but that was not where the real business was. The business came from tax attorneys and accountants.

After a few months of stressful and anxiety-ridden calls, my comfort zone expanded, and I was comfortable calling attorneys. But it wasn't easy to overcome my self-doubts and intimidation. I learned from reading, workshops, and experienced friends that all growth occurs outside the comfort zone.

Now as I enter new areas requiring a stretch of my comfort zone, I've learned to ask myself these questions. Use them to help you act outside your comfort zone. When deciding to take a risk, write your responses to these six questions.

## 1. What is the worst that can happen?

When I was asked to call on attorneys I was afraid I would:

- make a fool of myself

- be asked questions I didn't know how to answer

- be kicked out of their offices
- be embarrassed
- be told that I was wasting their time.

These are disaster fantasies. We think of the worst possible outcomes, whether they are realistic or not.

## 2. What is the likelihood of this happening?

Be realistic. The fear may distort your objectivity, but try. Often you will find the likelihood to be small.

## 3. If this did happen, could I live with the outcome?

If yes, go for it. If no, then strategize another plan. I decided yes, I could live with someone throwing me out of their office. I wouldn't enjoy it, it would be uncomfortable and emotionally painful, but I could live with it. I'd learn from my mistake and not make it again.

I once had an appointment with an attorney to solicit him as a center of influence. He was so hostile during the meeting that he stood behind his desk the whole time and never asked me to sit down. So I conducted the entire interview standing!

Did this experience leave me alive? Yes. Was it uncomfortable? Extremely. Did I learn from it? Yes—I was better prepared to deal with hostility and rejection.

### 4. What am I afraid won't happen?

Sometimes we fear what won't happen as much as what will happen. If I called on successful attorneys, I was afraid that I wouldn't get any referrals from these centers of influence, or that I wouldn't establish a positive image for myself and my firm. Repeat questions 2 and 3 to get past this particular point of resistance.

### 5. What are the benefits to my not taking this risk?

- It's comfortable at my current comfort zone. No pain.
- I don't have to think much. I can do my job on automatic pilot.
- I'm making enough money to get by.
- If I try something new, I might fail.
- I'm at the top of the heap right now.
- If I try something now I could fall on my face.
- I'm too old to change.

After you defend all your excuses, focus on the benefits to taking the risk.

### 6. What are the benefits to my taking this risk?

- I would learn new skills.

- I will feel better about myself because I'm trying something outside of my comfort zone.
- I could be wildly successful!

The late Doug Hooper, author of *You Are What You Think*, said "Anything that comes up in your life that will be to your betterment, say 'yes' to it immediately."

Don't think about how uncomfortable you will be, or that you've never tried this before, or that you don't think you can do it. Instead, work through the six questions, weigh the outcome, and more often than you think, you'll benefit from risking a yes.

*So began our trip to communication hell*

*Life's Lessons*

# *Even Communication Experts Miscommunicate*

"There's a program on virtual reality tonight at Stanford. Do you want to go?" my husband asked.

"I'm not sure. Tell me about it." I responded.

"Well, you put on these special goggles and gloves and you see a three dimensional picture of, say, a meadow. You reach out with the glove and you see your hand in this meadow. You turn your head and see one side of the meadow, or turn around to see what's behind you."

"That sounds fascinating. Let's go."

So began our trip to communication hell — a three-hour lecture by a droning researcher telling us about virtual reality. He even showed us a video of himself talking about virtual reality. Finally, we saw a few minutes of a video showing what you can see through the goggles.

This was hardly what I had in mind.

I'd expected to put on the goggles and gloves to experience virtual reality. How did we have such different expectations?

My husband described virtual reality in such a way that I assumed I'd be participating, not just listening to the experience. I thought that since it was a program at Stanford, we'd be in the lab where scientists were developing the technology. Wrong!

What could I have done to avoid this communication breakdown?

1. I could have asked a more direct question. Instead of "Tell me about it," I could have been more specific. "What will this program consist of?" would have helped me to have a clearer understanding.

2. I could have clarified my expectations, making sure that what I thought would happen was what my husband thought would happen. Then I could have made an informed choice about whether I wanted to listen to a three-hour lecture or not. If I had still chosen to attend, I would not have been so bored and disappointed.

It happens to all of us. The best we can do is prevent a trip to communication hell too often.

# *The Power of Commitment*

"Do or die!"

"Don't give up the ship!"

"Damn the torpedoes and full speed ahead!"

Military expressions are valuable during war when the price of failure is death. But they lose impact in our business or private life: failure is not quite as final. However, these sayings are based on a principle that applies to all aspects of our lives: commitment.

This commitment to one's goals is, for me, the most important rule for success. Without it, we fall prey to procrastination, bad habits, laziness, rationalization and a host of goal-defeating problems.

Commitment is a strong word—much stronger than "agreement." If I agree to meet you for a movie, I have three options—keeping my agreement, cancelling, or changing it. If I commit myself to meeting you, I will meet you no matter what.

Commitments often require sacrifice in order to

achieve a particular goal. If your goal is to be self-employed, you will probably have to sacrifice an active social life for awhile.

When I started my business I worked 14-hour days, six to seven days a week. I was totally committed to my goal. I dreamed of owning my own successful seminar company. I wanted to help others become the best they could be. I wanted to share my knowledge of the universal laws of success and make a living doing it.

I worked for someone else from 9-5, then I either designed, researched or presented a seminar in the evening. During lunch hours I made phone calls to prospective clients. On weekends I did my client correspondence.

I was busy, but happy. Sure, it was exhausting, but I was able to achieve my goal of being self-supporting in my own business in just one year, instead of the 2-3 I projected. I owe my success to my commitment to my goal.

I haven't achieved all my goals. At one time I wanted to be an interpreter at the United Nations. I took courses in Spanish, French and Japanese, but then I gave up. For many years I talked about learning to fly an airplane. I talked, but never took the first step. Looking back on my life, I can see the difference between goals I was committed to and ones I wasn't: I've succeeded at my committed goals.

When you are committed to your goals, attaining them is easier. Your choices are clearer. If your goal is to become the top salesperson in the company, then the choice between going home when everyone else does or staying an extra hour and to make ten cold calls may not be easy, but you know what you have to do, and you do it. If your goal is to lose 15 pounds, your choice between having a carrot or a piece of carrot cake becomes clearer. When you are not committed to your goals, your choices become hazy.

Being committed means doing whatever it takes. Commitment does not mean walking all over fellow workers or stabbing people in the back to attain your goals. It does mean making those extra phone calls or jogging around the block or working long hours even when you don't feel like it.

When the first Neiman-Marcus store burned to the ground in 1913, 5.5 years after it had opened, the owners could have easily collected the insurance money and gone off to do other things. But Herbert Marcus was the dreamer of the partners, and he persuaded them to collect the insurance money, canvas the family for additional funds and build a larger store.

They could have given up, but they didn't. Marcus kept the dream alive and did what it took to create an internationally known specialty store. Marcus was committed.

Lee Iacocca did what it took to save the ailing Chrysler Corporation. He even took only $1 a year in salary in order to leave the capital in the company. It worked. Now Chrysler is a successful automaker again. Iacocca was committed.

Being committed to our goals often isn't easy, and it takes considerable time and effort. That's why we make so few commitments and often have such trouble keeping them. Americans in general are impatient; we don't like to stand on line or wait; we want what we want right now. If everyone in America were promised a million dollars, tax free, for meditating one hour every day, from 5-6 a.m. for two years, I believe a high percentage would never collect the money. "Too much trouble," we'd say. That's the trouble with commitment—it's too much trouble.

Commitment requires strong self-discipline, and a persistent inner voice to urge us on. Self-discipline grows out of our commitment to our goals. Your inner voice may also conflict with your stated goals. This voice tries to fight commitments and wants to get out of them. It may say, "Oh, go home early. You've worked hard. You deserve it." Like a soldier facing the enemy, we face our own inner enemies— "I'll do it tomorrow," "I can't do it." When we accept a commitment, it should be with "do or die" determination, otherwise it's only a weak agreement. Real commitment takes courage, sacrifice, and perseverance.

If you are able to hang in there and work toward your dreams and your goals a little bit each day, you will have them. Commit yourself to the attainment of your goals, and develop the self-discipline to do what it takes. As an added benefit, you'll achieve the satisfaction and confidence that comes with your success. Don't let this be said of your life:

And nothing to look backward to with pride,
And nothing to look forward to with hope,
So now and never any different.

*Life's Lessons*

In war, in sports, in life, those without commitment to victory and success often create their own defeat. If we could see the meaning of "do or die" as does a soldier in battle, we would be victorious more often.

When you are committed, anything is possible.

"I'm just talking here — not saying anything."

## *Frivolous Talk*

*Frivolous: unworthy of serious attention; trivial; of little value.*

"And then he said...then she said...and then...and then..." and on and on. Have you been on the listening end of frivolous talk? You know it when you hear it, when someone prattles on and on about people you don't know, will never meet, and don't care about. Or when someone keeps talking and talking, saying little, perhaps even repeating themselves. A friend has a saying for this: "I'm just talking here — not saying anything."

Have you found yourself spending time involved in — or listening to — more frivolous talk than you'd care to? I know I have. But I also had an experience that made me realize how much frivolous talk I contribute.

I was attending a multiple-day off-site personal growth workshop. We'd been told that this workshop could be life-changing if we followed the guidance of our facilitators 100% while we were there. I'd enrolled because I wanted to have a life-changing experience, so I decided to participate full out — no holding back or deciding which processes I'd participate in, and which ones I wouldn't. I trusted these leaders, so I did the exercises fully.

The first day we were told there was to be no frivolous talk. In fact, there was to be no talk at all outside of our workshop room, other than to discuss logistics issues (e.g., car pooling). In other words, we were to be silent.

I was struck by how many times I'd think about chatting with my classmates about unimportant things—the weather, her pretty jacket, could he pass the salt. I saw how much "noise" I contributed. These things weren't really important, or I didn't need to speak to communicate them.

By forcing us into silence, we saw how little of our usual babble really needs to be said. When the silence was lifted a few days later, we were much quieter than we'd been before. When we did speak, it was to ask a deeper question, or to share a meaningful insight.

Although I've drifted back into some chatter, I talk less now than before.

Why don't you try it? You don't have to be silent, but think about what you say before you say it. Ask yourself "Does this really need to be said? Will it make a difference to my listener?" If not, then button it up!

# Are You Listening?

John Scully, former Apple Computer CEO, was asked by a reporter, "If you could change your title from Chief Executive Officer, what would you change it to?" He replied, "Chief Listener."

Tom Peters says "The highest compliment you can pay a customer is to listen."

Someone once told me, "Most of us are compulsive talkers and selective listeners. Instead we should be compulsive listeners and selective talkers."

We know that listening is important. But if we know it is so important, why don't we listen better?

Often we take others in our life for granted. We think we know what they're going to say. For example, consider the people you live with — your mate or your children. How do you listen to them? Now remember when you were first dating that special person in your life. I remember when I first dated my husband. I hung on his every word. He was fascinating. He was so intelligent. He knew so much. He was enthralling. Do you remember such a time? Do you listen the same way now? I work on it every day so I won't take him for granted and tune him out.

Listening well means showing people you're listening. In fact, you can tell when someone is listening. Remember what your parents always said: "Look at me when I'm talking to you." Your body language telegraphs your listening level.

However, some people are good at masking their disinterest. They make eye contact, nod and say "uh huh," even though they're not really listening. Their porch light is on, but nobody's home.

Another reason people don't listen well is because of biases and prejudices. I'm not proud to admit that I've allowed biases to get in the way of my listening well. I became acutely aware of this one day, when my then 15-year-old stepson, Alex, came home with an orange mohawk. When he spoke I worked to focus on his face, and ignore the distraction of the orange spikes on his head. I brought my attention back to his face, tried to listen, and was distracted again by his skeleton earring.

I realized that I had an opinion about young men who have punk haircuts that live in my house. It didn't bother me that his friends had green, purple, and bright red hair. It didn't even bother me that his girlfriend had a matching haircut! But it did bother me that this young man, living in my house, did. I saw a prejudice that I hadn't seen before.

We all have prejudices. We may not like someone's clothes, make up, speech patterns, or haircut. Yet we need to strive to listen to them fully.

Listening is a critical skill for success. It's not an

easy skill to acquire. We can all improve our listening. I hope you see the value in becoming the Chief Listener in your life.

*Life's Lessons*

**In life we sometimes run into dung**

*Life's Lessons*

# The Trail As Life

A few years ago I hiked to the former leper colony, Kalaupapa, on Molokai in Hawaii. It is a 3.5 mile strenuous trail down a 1600 ft. cliff with 26 switchbacks. I could hire a mule to negotiate the trail, but decided I'd get more out of the experience by walking.

I started early in the morning, before the sun had dried the trail from the night's rain. The trail was steep, with many mud holes and rocks. My companion and I followed another couple down the trail for awhile. As I watched where the woman ahead of me stepped, I thought "This trail is like life — each person chooses her own path."

- Watching the woman's foot prints, I then decided where to put my foot. If she sank into a mud hole or slid off a stone, I chose another place. If her foot stayed dry, I stepped in the same place. Don't we do that in life — watch others to learn what works or what doesn't? Then we change our actions accordingly.

- The most efficient path — straight over the edge of the cliff — would not have been a good idea, nor successful. Instead, we attained our success by constantly modifying our route through a series of turns. We must continually make adjustments, while still staying attuned to our goal.

- After 20 minutes, the couple in front moved out of sight. I had to stop trying to keep up with them and go at my own pace. Don't we sometimes catch ourselves comparing our progress to others? At some point we have to choose our own path.

- The mules traveled this trail every day, so of course they left their "calling cards" in the form of pungent dung. In life we sometimes run into dung. We have two choices:

    1) complain and whine to anyone who will listen, repeating to ourselves and others, "Why do I have to be around so much dung?" Or

    2) notice it's there, step in as little as possible, and move on.

- At each of the 26 switchbacks a signpost marked the switchback number. However, in the beginning were so focused on getting to the bottom, that we didn't notice half of the markers. Sometimes in life we're in such a hurry to reach the end, that we don't pause and notice and appreciate the markers or milestones.

*Life's Lessons*

- When we slowed down or stopped we noticed beautiful views of the sea below, small flowers, birds, insects, animals, and sights that we wouldn't have seen if we had kept our heads down and focused only on the muddy trail.

- Although the trail was predominantly downhill, occasionally there was a rise before we descended again. Like the trail, life has its ups and downs.

- Because the trail was slick, we couldn't move quickly. Instead, we had to be flexible and make judgements every step of the way.

- Once, we rounded a switchback and came face-to-face with a 200-pound wild boar. You never know what will be around life's next corner, so stay alert. You also never know when you'll encounter a 200-pound boar.

We could have taken the mules. But we wouldn't have seen the same sights, felt the trail beneath us, met the boar, or had the same experience. There are easier ways to the same destination, but they're not the same journey.

*When you are focused on the activity your primal brain takes over*

# Leadership Walk

It is easy to intellectualize about leadership, risk taking, and team communication when you are safely in an air-conditioned training room. But when you are put into an activity that forces you to act — often without thinking — your true behaviors come out.

When you are focused on the activity your primal brain takes over. There's no room for theory or academic concepts. You are stripped of much ability for strategic thinking. Your body thinks you are in danger and whatever is deeply entrenched in you comes out, through your words, actions, or both. Sometimes you're not even aware of what you said or did until the debrief. You get to look at your true beliefs and abilities so you can work at changing them if needed.

Before leading a series of leadership workshops for groups at the spa/resort Miraval, in the mountains above Tucson, AZ, I decided to put myself through the outdoor challenges I was going to ask my participants to experience. The first was The Leadership Walk.

I and two other women met Chris, our leader. He was an affable, insightful outdoor man, who had previously run Outward Bound experiences.

We began by all being blindfolded. Then we were put one behind each other as Chris led us around the grounds. While we could talk to each other, Chris was mute. The person behind Chris had to explain what was happening so we could walk safely and comfortably over our route.

Susan was the first person behind Chris. She was communicative and confident, but when we were led down some stairs, I found myself faltering because I wasn't clear on what to expect. I asked, "Susan, can you give us an estimate of how high each step is, and let us know when we're on flat ground again?" When she did, it was easier to follow.

Periodically, Chris would change the leader. I was the last to take my turn at the head of the line. By this time, we had run out of pavement, and were being taken down a hill with crudely made steps, full of rocks. I had to descend carefully, while announcing to my followers what was coming up for them.

The woman immediately behind me, Sally, seemed particularly inept at this exercise. Although I would announce "Six-inch step down ahead" she would shriek as if surprised when a step later she reached this point. She was extremely cautious, often saying "hold on" even through easy turf. I found myself getting irritated with her, and having to force myself to be patient.

Part way through, it occurred to me that perhaps I wasn't leading in a way that made her comfortable. So I asked both women "What could I do differently to make it easier to follow? Am I giving enough details? Anything I should do differently?" They couldn't come up with anything.

Finally, when we reached the bottom of the hill, Chris let us take off our blindfolds. Looking back, I saw how steep the hill was. However, I was never frightened because I could feel the strength in Chris' hand as he led us downhill, and I felt him stop when something difficult was ahead.

## Lessons learned

- If a leader isn't as effective as s/he could be for you, ask if s/he could modify his/her style.

- Ask how your own leadership style is working. Too often when our followers don't react as we expect, we blame them. Perhaps we first need to see if they need to be lead differently.

- Once you've experienced a leader's caring and competence, trust that they will take care of you. If you are always blaming or second-guessing them, you'll get nowhere.

*Life's Lessons*

**Sometimes you have to go down to then go up**

*Life's Lessons*

# Borrowing Courage

The Climbing Wall experience at Miraval was the most difficult for me physically. Not only am I afraid of heights, but I don't have a lot of upper-body strength.

Chris, our facilitator, gave the six of us an overview of the activity, harnesses and special climbing shoes. Wendy, a 30-something woman from Chicago, sat next to me. When Chris asked why we were here to do this activity, she admitted she wasn't sure she wanted to do it. She wasn't feeling well, and was afraid of heights. I suggested she might just get in the gear to see what it felt like, and she could quit at any point. She donned the equipment as we looked at the wall and the belaying apparatus.

We would be climbing in pairs, tethered via a 4' rope. I liked this idea. If I was paired with someone who stealthily sped up the wall like Spiderman, I would have felt inept. I know, we shouldn't compare ourselves to others, but sometimes you can't help it.

When Chris asked who wanted to pair up, Wendy said she'd like me to be her partner.

As we looked at the wall, Chris asked Wendy and me to hook into the belay line to show how this was going to work. Little did I know that meant we were going first!

He had us climb up 3 to 4 feet, then hang off the wall so the belayers could understand their job. Then he had us repel back to the ground. Easy enough.

Now, to climb for real. He explained that we should go as far as we wanted. I hadn't really thought if I wanted to go to the top, but decided why not? We started to climb. It quickly became apparent that not only did I not have great upper body strength, but the legs I thought were so strong couldn't boost me if the step was too high. So I utilized my ground crew — the belayers and onlookers — early on. "Do you see a foothold for me?" I learned that sometimes I had to go back down a step in order to reach better footing. The belayers never failed to help me find a hand or foothold.

While I was fighting my own challenges, Wendy was too. She would frequently pause and say, "I can't do this." I would cheer her on, not only for her sake, but whatever I said to her, I needed to hear too. "You're doing great. Look how far we've come. You can do it." At one point I heard her familiar cry, "I can't do this." I looked over to see her moving her foot higher at the same time! She had no idea she was exclaiming she couldn't do something while she was doing it!

About 20 feet up, I paused. I was exhausted. My legs were wobbly and my arms were fatigued. I looked down. "Holy crap!" I thought. "This is too high. I don't think I have the physical strength for this. I think I should stop and go down." I looked at Wendy. She was a little ahead of me. If Wendy, who is also afraid of heights, and not in great shape, and continually yelling she can't do it, can go further than I am, then I can do it! I took a deep breath, focused, and grabbed for the next handhold.

The last part was the most difficult. The final step to touch the top was a killer. I tried and fell back, caught by the belayers. I tried again. Finally, I took a deep breath, mustered all my determination, stepped high, let loose with one hand, and touched the top! Yeah! Victory! Wendy soon followed. We celebrated with high fives, before the belayers let us back down.

Back on the ground, Wendy said to me, "Thanks for loaning me some of your courage." "What do you mean?" I asked. She said, "I know you are as afraid of heights as I am. Yet you not only kept climbing, you encouraged me, too. I don't think I could have made it without your encouragement and watching your courage." Wow. I hugged her, "Thank you, Wendy."

## Lessons learned

- Just put on the gear. You can always take it off. But if you don't put on the gear, you're never going to get in the game.

- Utilize your ground crew — your support team — to coach you to success.

- Sometimes you have to go down to then go up. Be willing to step back to pursue a better path.

- Listen when you encourage others, as it might be something you need to hear for yourself.

*Life's Lessons*

- When you get doubtful that you'll succeed, breathe, ground yourself and focus.

- By stretching your own limits, you are inspiring to others. They will borrow your courage, without your even knowing it.

# Lessons From a Horse

My experience with horses is minimal. My good experiences (riding on a beach or in the mountains) were offset by two deeply imbedded negative ones. The latest was when I was invited to ride a friend's horse at his ranch. He held the horse while I tried to mount it. Unfortunately, we didn't notice the horse was uphill, so I couldn't pull myself up and over his back. I fell back, badly spraining my ankle in the process, experiencing searing pain. The other time my slightly-older then 11-year-old cousin spurred the horse we were riding to take off in a gallop — with me grabbing tightly around her waist, coming down hard on the back of the saddle with each landing. I was terrified of falling off this stampeding animal, while she laughed wickedly.

Needless to say, I brought some psychological baggage to this activity at Miraval. The trainers added to my trepidation by reminding us that these 1500-pound animals could kick and do real pain and damage. With that, they instructed us on how to not get hurt, and more to the point of this exercise, how to let the horse know who was boss.

The first activity was to groom the horse. My horse, Monty, was parallel to the fence. I had to first get Monty to face the fence perpendicular. We were clearly instructed not to approach from behind, or we'd get kicked. Instead, approach him at the shoulder. Then I pushed Monty on the flank to where I wanted. Luckily, Monty cooperated.

As I touched him, I talked to him. The trainer told me not to talk to him, because I was trying to schmooze him. She said I did that with people, tried to get them to like me so they'd do what I wanted. She said it didn't matter if he liked me, he would do what I wanted if I made it clear that was what I expected. So I stopped talking to him and focused on telegraphing my desires differently.

Now to clean his hooves. This was tricky, as I had to get Monty to raise each hoof, then I had to hold it while I cleaned it. Meanwhile, he tried to put his foot down. To get Monty to raise his hoof, I had to squeeze him in a special spot near his ankle. I had trouble finding it. I felt incompetent. Finally, I found it; he raised his foot for a second, then put it down. I struggled to find the spot again. This time, when his foot raised, I caught it. Yes! It seemed to take forever to get the first one done, and I had 3 more to do!

This incompetent feeling was familiar and unpleasant. It's often hard to try something completely new because we typically didn't do it well at first, so feel inept. It takes a lot of willingness to feel like a beginner — and usually incompetent — to try new tasks and experiences. The challenge is to hang in through the incompetent period. Ideally, we begin to actually embrace that feeling because then we know we're stretching, growing, and experiencing something new, not sticking with the boring tried and true.

After the hoof cleaning, next was brushing. A simple-enough sounding task, but I had to be fully present to make sure Monty wasn't startled and kick me. I had to be clear with my focus and intention, and fully present and paying attention. No daydreaming here.

How often do we not pay attention in life? Especially in a seemingly no-brainer task like driving? Aren't the potential repercussions of not being present while driving similar to the threat of being kicked by a 1-ton horse? Yet we become so complacent, we don't think of the ramifications of not paying attention to common tasks, even when we understand the dangers of allowing our attention to wane.

## *Lessons learned*

- To embrace the feeling of incompetence, rather than avoiding it. Not that one should try to be incompetent, but rather be willing to try new things, be a beginner, and be OK if you don't do well at first.

- You don't have to feel people need to like you to follow you. You just need to be clear on what you want, and focus your energy and intention on it.

*Life's Lessons*

**I watched the mostly 20-somethings scamper up the 30-foot pole in seconds**

*Life's Lessons*

# *Taking a Stand*

I was tired when I joined the afternoon group for this activity — climbing a 30-foot telephone pole then stepping on the top, and leaping off (belayed with a harness and rope all the time). I hadn't planned to do it at all, as I had a massage scheduled. But after bonding with several of the participants during another experience, I decided to change my appointment so I could join them in this.

The storm clouds were coming in over the Arizona sky, so I hoped that if I procrastinated long enough the rains would come and I could bail out. When the facilitator, Kevin, asked for people to choose their order, I took the last spot. I didn't even have enough energy to take a turn as a belayer. I just sat on a log and cheered people on.

I watched the mostly 20-somethings scamper up the 30-foot pole in seconds, seemingly leaping on top and stand at attention. One woman was so confident, she did a one-legged yoga pose. A young, buff guy was going to do a handstand, but instead opted for another yoga pose. Most people dismounted by falling backward, the easiest way to get off the pole.

Finally, it was my turn. Would I do it or pass? Kevin yelled my number. I paused while I made my decision.

I thought, "Drat, I guess I have to do it to see if I want to include it in the leadership seminars I'll do here. OK. Put on the harness and helmet."

I climbed the 6-foot ladder, then the pole, reasonably easily, considering my lack of energy. I guess adrenaline had kicked in. I was OK as long as I didn't look down. Then, at the top, I ran out of foot/hand rungs to hang onto. The only thing left was to hang on to the dinner-plate-sized disk on the top, which rotates! I grabbed on, which meant I had to hang over the top so I could balance to get one foot on the disk. Looking straight down 30 feet was unnerving. But I placed one foot on the disk. Now, how to get the other one up? This was hard, as I had to shift my weight onto the top foot and balance while bringing up the other foot. Breathe, focus, OK, now! Did it!

I was doubled over as I hung on to the plate with both hands with both feet on top. Now to stand up — with nothing to hang on to or with which to steady myself. Talk about faith! I took a deep breath and asked myself "What are you willing to take a stand for?" The answer came immediately: My new life — the life I was creating in part by facilitating leadership retreats at this resort! I stood up confidently. Yippee!

I looked around the beautiful high desert, and enjoyed watching the storm clouds against the prominent peaks. Stunning. As I prepared to dismount, Kevin asked, "What are you leaping into?" I replied, "I'm leaping into my new life!" With that I turned on the disk — a 9.9-degree of difficulty — and leapt off the pole!

## Lessons learn

- Even if you don't have energy to participate full out, you can still be supportive of others by showing up and doing what you can.
- If you are committed, it doesn't matter how tired you are.
- Isn't so much of life just putting one foot in front of (or above) the other?
- Take your time if you are scared. Remind yourself of what you need: breathe, focus.
- When faced with a very difficult task, remind yourself of something that inspires you. It will give you the energy and focus to take a stand.
- You can accomplish amazing things when you are balanced, clear on what you want, focused and grounded.
- With every action, be clear in what you want. I was clear I wanted to leap into my new life with energy, courage, passion and clarity.

*Life's Lessons*

**For what are you willing to go out on a limb?**

*Life's Lessons*

# Trust Your Guides

While walking the 5 minutes from the meeting place to the activity area, Chris, our facilitator, instructed us to discuss with a partner for what in our lives were we willing to go out on a limb. What did it mean to us to go out on a limb? What prevents us from doing so for things we believe in?

By the time we reached the activity area, we were psychologically ready for this challenge. We counted off to determine our climbing order. I choose 5, in the middle of the pack.

This activity required us to climb a 10-foot ladder then a pole about 25 feet high, with footholds. An 18-inch thick log is attached to two upright poles. When you reach the log, you step out on it, letting go of the vertical pole, and walk across to the other side. Sounds easy, yes?

I watched the first people go across, with varying levels of confidence. The biggest challenge for most was the transition from the vertical to the horizontal log. Letting go of the vertical seemed very difficult.

When I worked as ground crew, I asked others what they wanted from us, how we could support them. They generally replied, "Be encouraging." I countered, "What does that look and sound like to you." They'd think for a minute, then gave specific phrases to say when it looked like they were faltering.

After my turn as ground crew, I awaited my turn by practicing walking on similar large logs lying around the activity area. I noticed that walking on a round log wasn't easy, even when it was on the ground. I practiced breathing, centering and focusing, then walking on the logs to see what pace seemed easiest to keep my balance. I wanted to get this in my muscle memory so it was second nature when I was 25 feet in the air.

Finally, it was my turn. I hooked my harness into the belayers' line. I told the ground crew what to say to support me. I hugged Chris. And I started climbing.

The vertical climb was almost easy, even though the foot/hand holds were 18 inches apart. I placed one foot above the other and soon I was at the horizontal log. I maneuvered my way out onto the log, still clutching the pole. I took a deep breath, grounded myself, and focused on the far pole. I stuck my free hand out and took a step forward. But my other hand was fused to the pole. I tried again, breathe, ground, focus, step forward. The hand did not let go. I tried talking to it, telling it I was safe and that it could let go. Nothing.

I yelled to Chris "Why is it so hard to let go?"

"Why don't you want to let go?"

"Because it's safe and secure. I know I won't fall."

"And why would you want to let go?"

"Because staying here is boring. I'd be stuck. I know what it's like. The only way to grow is to move forward and let go."

"What do you need to let go?"

"I need to breathe, ground and focus on where I want to go — the other pole." Noticing two knot holes side by side on the other pole, I said "Hey, Chris, did you know there was a face on the other pole?"

"Really. I've been up there lots of times and I haven't noticed a face. What does it look like?"

"An owl."

"What's the owl saying to you?"

"Breath. Focus. Let go." So I did. I let go and began crossing the log. "He's saying to stay focused on him, that he'll get me through this. I can do anything I want if I just breathe, ground, focus, let go and take action." Now I was at the other pole! The owl had walked me through it! I kissed the face, and prepared to dismount.

Chris yelled, "Before you dismount, what do you want to leave in the desert here?"

"I want to leave the parts of my life that no longer serve me, are no longer working. I will leave them here, as I don't need them anymore." And with that, I leaned off the log backwards, knowing my belayers would lower me safely to the ground.

## *Lessons learned*

- Ask others specifically what they need. What does support look and sound like? Then give them what they requested.

- Practice first. When trying something way outside your comfort zone, find a way to simulate the experience so you can see what works and what you have to modify to be successful.

- Watch what worked for others and where they had difficulty. Create a strategy for how you'll deal with difficulty if you experience it.

- Ask for the support you want. Tell people specifically what you need to feel supported.

- Let go. This is so easy to say and so hard to do when you don't feel safe. Even when your mind knows you're safe, you body doesn't always buy it.

- Focus on something other than your fear. Create a dialog with a guiding force if that helps.

- Leave behind anything that no longer serves you. You don't need it anymore, so let it go.

# Hard-Won Lessons

I'm afraid of heights, remember? I'd watched 3 previous pairs traverse a cable 25 feet in the air, so I saw what worked — and what didn't.

The task was for each of the pair to climb up a different telephone pole, then step out on a Y-shaped cable, all the while safely belayed by a team below, so you couldn't fall. Once both people reached the mid-point of the Y, they were to figure out how to reach a rope that was hanging at the base of the Y.

Before mounting the ladder, I asked my belaying team to remind me of some key phrases if I got stuck.

1. Breathe. When I get stressed, I forget to breathe.//
2. Ground. Take a moment to ground myself with that breath.
3. Put my butt in, not out. This was critical for the success of others, yet I saw how our bodies naturally want to do the opposite.

Since I'm not that athletic, I took my time climbing the pole. When I arrived at the cable, I looked over at

Steve, a personal trainer and the stranger with whom I was partnered with for this activity. He was standing on the cable, leaning against the pole, with his arms crossed. Steve had apparently scampered up the pole in seconds. I yelled across to him, "What are you doing?" "Waiting for you," he replied. I got irritated. I thought he was being condescending. I didn't need him waiting for me!

I stepped onto the cable. Whoa! This was not as easy as my predecessors made it look. Even though my mind knew I was safely belayed and I could not hurt myself, my legs didn't get the message. They shook uncontrollably. I had to talk to them as if they were small children: "Legs, it's OK. Your team has you safely belayed. You can't fall. You'll be fine. Stop shaking." Finally my legs got the message.

Now to move along the cable to the center. How did the others make it look so easy? Even knowing the key to making it work, it was hard to actually *do* what my mind knew to do. The key behavior was counter-intuitive, and I had to make my body do things that it did not want to do!

I talked myself through it: "Breathe. Focus. Move forward. Butt in, not out. Trust your team. Lean forward." Later the ground crew said they were amazed that I kept my feet moving forward, even though my legs were shaking.

As I neared the safety of the supported mid-point, Steve reached out to help me. I noticed I resented this, even though I knew he was trying to be helpful. I wanted to do it myself, and didn't need his help, thank you very much.

"Now how do we get the rope that is 15 feet away?" I asked, hoping he'd say, "I'll do it." No such luck. "Let's try something different than what the others did," he offered. "But we know what they did worked" I countered. "Well, one of us could grab the rope. We both don't have to go," I suggested, again hoping he'd volunteer. "You're closer," he pointed out. Drat! He was right. "But you're obviously more facile at shimmying along this cable" I negotiated. "Whatever you want" he turned it back to me.

I thought for a moment. It would be easier to have him do it. I could stay safely at the mid-point where it would be easy to watch him and cheer him on. Or I could stretch my limits and try to go the 15 feet and grab the rope. Sigh. The latter would be a better growth experience for me. Don't you sometimes get tired of these darn growth experiences?

"OK. I'll do it. But let's come up with a plan. Hold on to me as far as you can to give me stability." He held on, but I lost my balance and almost fell off the cable. He helped me up. We adjusted our position, and moved along the cable together halfway, then I reached out and caught the rope. Success!

After taking in the success, we "flew" down to the ground with the help of our belaying team gently lowering us to the ground.

## Lessons learned

- Analyze what worked for others, but use it for information, not necessarily as your strategy.

- Ask for what you need and want for support.
- Be present. Instead of ignoring my shaking legs, I noticed them and talked them into calm.
- Trust your team. I had to do something that was counter-intuitive in order to be successful. That was a big risk. But I could not have been successful without trusting them.
- Don't get hooked by someone else's progress. They're on their own path and have different things to experience and learn. So Steve's apparent ease needn't have affected my lessons.
- Know what you need. I allowed myself to pause, tell myself to breathe and other messages.
- Don't take the easy way out. There's no growth in playing it safe.
- Take risks when you know you can trust your ground crew. You can fly if you play your cards right!
- The most important lesson: Only help when there is a request for help or when you've asked if someone wants help and they accept. I, like Steve, am generally a helpful person. Yet I experienced how condescending it can feel to be helped when you don't want or need someone's help. This is a biggie.

# *Being a Conscious Conversationalist*

Being a conscious conversationalist is critical to a long-term relationship, whether with a coworker, customer, or friend — at least for me. I've encountered many people who are conversationally challenged. Since it is doubtful your friends or colleagues will volunteer that you are an inept conversationalist, as a public service I thought I'd delineate some of the most common conversational culprits.

- *Taking most of the air time.* A conscious conversationalist will be aware of approximately how much of the talk time she is taking and when it begins to feel like she's monopolized the conversation, turn the focus on the other person. You can simply say, "I've been talking non stop. Tell me (something relevant to them)."

- *Repeating yourself.* If you aren't paying enough attention to what you are saying that you repeat yourself, how much do you think the other person will feel you're listening to them?

- *Turning the focus back to you.* I had a recent conversation with someone I'd just met. He regularly turned the conversation to himself. We were talking about the world's awareness of US affairs. Since I hadn't shared much by this point, I said "When I was in Malaysia last summer, I was amazed at how many of my contacts watched the Democratic convention on CNN." His next line was not, "What did you make of that?" or "What did they think of US politics?" or "What were you doing in Malaysia?" No. It was, "A friend has a manufacturing plant in Malaysia that makes dolls. He wants to hire me to do some work for him. Look it up at www.XXXXX.com."

- *Not asking relevant follow-up questions.* This same caller said he thought I was fascinating. Which I found odd because I had said barely 10 sentences after 30 minutes into the call. He could have found out about me by asking relevant follow-up questions to my comments, as I illustrated above. If both parties merely jump into a conversation with their own stories or thoughts, it's as if two people are having sequential monologues. To really get to know someone's thoughts, values, and opinions, you have to dig deeper into what they share.

- *Delving into unimportant details.* Your conversation partner doesn't need to know every detail of your story. Try to keep it pithy but still include relevant information. Most people could cut their chatter by half, if not 2/3, if they focused on just key elements to get their thought across. If someone wants more detail they'll ask. Better to error on the side of pithiness.

- *Interrupting.* When someone is talking, let them finish their story or thought. Of course, this is a challenge if they are going on and on and on about something of no interest to you. If you need to interrupt to clarify something, do so with, "I need to interrupt before you go on because I'm confused about..." You are interrupting to better understand what they are sharing, not to change the subject or focus the conversation back on you.

- *Not letting the other person answer your questions.* If you ask a question and as soon as your conversation partner starts sharing, you interject, "That happened to me, too! Let me tell you about it..." you are showing you don't really care to know about them.

- *Too many non sequiturs.* If you can't stay with the thread of the conversation and are continually changing the subject (often back to focusing on you), it is difficult to have an in-depth discussion. Yes, we all get reminded of something that is a little off the subject, and if you find your stream of consciousness takes you far afield, you can acknowledge that, "This is a tad off topic, but your comment reminded me of....." Or if you have more to share on the topic but your partner has gone on a tangent, simply say, "I had another thought I wanted to share on ....."

- *Short or curt answers.* While I believe in being pithy, curt or short answers are not attractive. If you don't want to talk about something, simply say, "I'd rather not go there right now." or "I'll tell you about that after we know each other a bit better."

- *Being unaware of what might be of interest to the listener.* If you babble on about things that your listener probably doesn't care about, then they lose interest not only in the conversation, but with developing a relationship with you. If your side of the dialog is filled with information about your children, grandchildren, first job, high school, your friends (and your friends' children and grandchildren), you'll soon lose your listener. Try to edit in your mind before spewing out whatever crosses your thoughts. Think, "Would this likely interest my listener?" and delete anything that you can't say yes to, no matter how much interest it holds for you. Once someone knows and cares about you, they are more interested in the broader spectrum of your life. But not at first.

- *Boasting.* If you are the hero of every story, it gets tedious to listen to you. If you are proud of something, you can start off with, "I'm so excited..."

But to keep interjecting stories where you are the champion will earn you the title of bore.

- *Name dropping incessantly.* This same caller told me how he had put up a Facebook page and a bunch of politicians had asked to be his friend. He named the politicians, none of whom I recognized. If you have to name drop regularly to show how important you are, you're really telegraphing your insecurities.

We all have some poor conversational habits, myself included. The key is to get some honest feedback from those who care about you. Ask them to be candid with you. Show them the above list and ask if you are guilty of any of the items. And engage them to help you increase your awareness by saying something like "TMI (too much information)" if you start to go into unimportant details.

This will yield not only stronger friendships, but more solid relationships with colleagues and customers.

*Life's Lessons*

> "Words not only affect us temporarily — they change us"

# *The Power of Our Words*

Author David Riesman said, "Words not only affect us temporarily — they change us."

Do you remember when someone's words hurt you? Perhaps they called you "skinny," "stupid," "four eyes," or "ugly." It probably felt like someone slapped you.

How about when someone's words made you feel great, such as "You're wonderful," "That was an excellent job," "I love you."? I'll bet you can remember the exact words and tone from each memory.

Words can comfort when we're feeling sad, inspire us to take action, acknowledge us for a job well done, humiliate us, make us laugh, stimulate our thoughts, educate us, or incite violence.

Words have created fist fights, divorces, murders, and wars. To "exchange words" has always expressed aggression and conflict. However, a high compliment is, "She keeps her word."

Our words are so much more powerful than we realize. We take our words for granted, because we say so many in a day.

How are you using your words? Are you aware of what you say to others? Or do words just fall out of your mouth?

A few years ago I had a deep epiphany. I'd found myself becoming increasingly negative, cynical, and judgmental. This was not great for someone who's supposed to be motivating others! I was wrestling with whether or not my words made any difference to my audiences. I felt like it didn't matter if I showed up for a speech or not.

The turning point came when I repeatedly had trouble dragging myself out of bed on days of I was to deliver a speech. "Drat! Do I have to give another motivational talk?" I knew I was in real trouble.

Something dramatic needed to change immediately. At the recommendation of a mentor, I enrolled in an intensive nine-day personal growth seminar. Over the last 20 years I'd taken many personal and professional development seminars, but this one was more powerful than all the others put together.

## *The Change*

I emerged from the program profoundly changed. Hearing my fellow participants share their fears, doubts, and regrets during the seminar, I saw that much of the pain we'd all spoken about in the seminar was created because of words directed at us, or words we'd said to loved ones, and wished we hadn't, or words of love we wish we'd said, but didn't. Have you ever experienced pain because of words said — or unsaid?

I began to examine the impact of words in my life. My insight was a deepened awareness of how powerful our words are. I'd known intellectually most of my life, but I'd never understood it at such a deep emotional level.

You see, much of my life I'd used words to disconnect me from others. Funny, since I'd been a communication major in college, and I've been spreading the gospel of communication for the past 15 years as a professional speaker and author. Yet I saw how clumsy, and often cruel, I'd been with my words. I used words to create a wall around me so others couldn't get close. If they weren't close, they couldn't hurt me.

Have you ever built a wall to keep out pain?

## Sticks and Stones

Have you ever believed the children's chant, "Sticks and stones can break my bones, but words can never hurt me"? I'd thought I believed it. But now I admit how deeply others' words have affected me. And, I see how my sometimes sharp words have affected others.

I created a phrase to help me remember this lesson: words can cut, words can heal. After the nine-day workshop, I was determined to focus on healing words.

I emerged feeling that I had more empathy. I felt like I was oozing with love and compassion. I was now more vulnerable and sensitive to pain — mine and others — than ever in my life. I saw how I'd clumsily caused others pain, often without knowing it. I felt I was now on the right path. I was cured! Or so I thought.

Have you ever thought you were changed, only to be given proof that you weren't?

## Cured?

Two months after the workshop, I had lunch with three close friends. Midway through the meal, one friend told us of a minor indiscretion she'd made on email — she'd innocently emailed to someone she didn't know from someone else's distribution list.

As the techno-expert at the table, I decided she needed to see her faux pas: "How could you do that? How crass. That's like sending electronic junk mail. You should never send email to anothers' distribution list. This is a violation of cyber etiquette." And on and on. I was stern. I was adamant. I was insensitive. She burst into tears.

I'd become so numb to my words' effect on others, I hadn't imagined she'd react this way. In retrospect, I can see how easily I'd hurt others, often without being aware of it.

Here I was, fresh from the most profound personal work I had ever done, supposedly full of love and light, and I was belittling one of my dearest friends. My words were still causing others pain, still cutting when I wanted to be healing. I had so much work left to do in my quest for sensitivity and caring. This oozing with love and compassion was not going to be as easy as I thought.

Even with awareness, putting my new sensitivity into action isn't easy. The concept of "words can cut, words can heal" is easy enough to grasp. Yet it is not so easy to institute every day, in every conversation, especially in times of stress, tension and change.

Because of our busy lives we don't often think through "How might my comment leave the receiver? Feeling respected, or diminished?" Feeling better about himself, or worse?

A while ago one of my clients asked me to work with a supervisor, Deb, whom they wanted to promote. Yet she had some communication habits that kept her unpromoted. One of these habits was the manner in which she communicated policy and process changes to her staff. After a management meeting she would return to her area and tell her staff, "You're not going to believe what those bozos want us to do now." As you would guess, her staff was resistant to the changes.

During my discussion with Deb, she came to understand the power she held. She hadn't seen herself as a leader, so didn't see how her words were undermining management's efforts. She quickly understood, and began to communicate management's decisions — even ones she didn't like — positively.

You may face situations similar to Deb's. In any business, there are changes. There will be many times when you will have to explain these new processes to your associates. You can choose to explain them positively, or you could add your own editorial comments. For your success, the success of your associates, and of the company, I encourage you to think through your words before sharing them.

## Manager's Words Have Added Weight

If you manage people, your words have much more weight than you may realize. Jak, shared a recent realization. Although for 30 years he'd worked as a manager, executive, and now CEO, he hadn't really understood the long-lasting impact that his words had on his staff.

He had became frustrated by all the hubbub generated by a seemingly offhand comment he'd made to one of his staff. He'd thought he had gently teased her about a mistake she'd made. She, however, took his comments to heart, was very upset, and discussed it with dozens of coworkers. She felt he was focusing on her mistakes rather than on what she did well. She was concerned about losing her job.

He told me there was never a question of her losing her job. He saw how deeply his offhanded words had affected her. He became more vigilant about his comments before he opened his mouth, not only with her, but with everyone at his office. He hadn't fully understood how powerful his words were, especially with his staff.

## Humor Can Backfire

Jak had been trying to be funny about the mistake. Sometimes we use humor to lighten up a situation, but it backfires.

Are we saying things to our customers or associates that would be better off unsaid? Are we phrasing things as positively as we could?

When I was shopping for disability insurance. a financial planner friend recommended an agent. When I called the agent, he asked if he could send me a proposal rather than making the hour's drive to see me. This was unusual, but I said "Sure."

After I received the proposal, we discussed it over the phone. Having come from the insurance industry, I asked, "Why did you choose to quote these particular companies?"

He responded, "Because they give me the best contract," which meant that he got the highest commission from them.

"Why aren't you quoting some of the large companies known for their disability policies?" I asked.

"Because if biggest were best, Miss America would weigh 300 pounds!"

He said this to a woman with a weight problem! He had no idea he'd been insulting. I bought from someone else.

I've spent much of my life trying to be funny — at other people's expense. Have you ever done that?

I've teased people about their touchy areas. When they didn't take it well, I accused them of being too sensitive and unable to take a joke. For all my tough bravado, the truth was, I could dish it out, but I couldn't take it. I was more sensitive than I let on. With my new awareness, I realized that I'd been given this lesson ten years earlier, but I didn't know it. It happened when I was a participant in an image seminar.

I was looking for a little brush up on the nuances of dressing for success. I enrolled in a day-long image seminar, led by, well, let's just call him "Danté."

All 40 of us were instructed to bring three outfits for critique: casual chic, power business, and elegant evening. Confidently, I changed into my first outfit, casual chic: low heeled navy pumps with matching hose, tailored navy wool trousers, red silk shirt, a navy cashmere sweater, and a red and navy silk scarf.

I stood before the group for my critique. On a scale of 1-10, with 10 being "you belong in Vogue Magazine" and 1 being "you should move back in with your mother so she can dress you," Danté's score for this outfit: 5. He added, "You look like the captain of your bowling team." I was hurt. But I didn't let on.

I thought "I've got the other categories aced. I know I'll do better on them."

Second round—power business. I changed into my Evan Picone suit with silk blouse, pumps, matching hose, and silk scarf accented by "take charge" gold earrings.

Danté's assessment: 4. I thought: "I'm going the wrong way." He added "You look like a supervisor for Ma Bell making $18,000 a year." I was crushed.

We took a lunch break. Although I was near tears, I bolstered myself by thinking "I'm going to nail Elegant Evening." A student fashion designer friend had designed my gown and I'd made it. When I'd worn it to formal events I'd received lots of compliments. This was a sure thing.

I spent much of my lunch break redoing my makeup and putting my hair into an upsweep. I was lookin' good.

As I stood before the group, I knew Danté would be stunned by my sophistication. I awaited his pronouncement: 2. "You look like a librarian on her night out. Or a nun's idea of sexy."

I was devastated. I left so paralyzed that I couldn't go shopping alone for two years. I'd allowed him to strip me of my confidence about my appearance and taste.

Remember Riesman's quote "Words not only affect us temporarily—they change us." Danté's words changed me so that I was incapacitated. Words can cut, words can heal. Today, I see that my lesson was: "Humor, at someone else's expense, can cut more deeply than we'll ever know."

## Compare

Compare Danté's comments with an equally harsh sounding statement that Robert's mentor made to him at the end of 1994. June Anderson, the mentor, had reviewed his financial statements for his two-year-old business and his forecast for the next 12 months. After much discussion, she told him, "Robert, you don't have a business, you have a hobby." Ouch. It was like having a bucket of ice water poured on him. It was hard to hear those words, but it woke him up. He immediately closed that business and joined forces with a colleague on a much more lucrative venture.

How are June's words much different from Danté's. Danté's words were public, said to entertain, not to help.

Previous to and following June's words she had acknowledged Robert's talents and the parts of his business that he did well. There was none of that with Danté. June followed up with specific areas to help Robert. Again, none of that with Danté. And finally, their demeanors were different. Danté's was arrogant and superior; June's was caring, and interested in Robert's success.

Intellectually I know that we have the power to ignore others' disempowering words, or discredit the source, or simply reframe them more positively to serve us.

## *Well-Meaning Words*

Sometimes even well-meaning words affect us negatively. A woman shared an example of this. Her granddaughter had died recently, and a friend of hers said, "I know just how you feel. Last year, my dog died."

Although she told herself that her friend was trying to empathize and comfort her, it hurt that her friend thought that losing a dog was the same as losing a granddaughter. As much as she told herself that her friend was trying to be helpful by expressing the sadness of losing someone close to her, she still cried as she told the story.

Several years ago, I served as Convention Logistics Chair for my professional association. My overall responsibilities included a multitude of things, from recruiting over 100 volunteers, to overseeing each session's room setup. I was accountable for hundreds of details that would set the meeting's tone and ensure the smoothness of the sessions.

I had flown cross country twice, at my own expense, to attend committee meetings. I had spent countless hours on my duties.

On the last day of the convention, the president called a handful of key volunteers on stage. He'd intended to acknowledge us in front of our 1600 peers.

He said a few things about each volunteer and what each had contributed to the convention. When he came to me he said just two sentences I will never forget.

*"Rebecca did the little things. If no one else would do it, we knew Rebecca would."*

I winced. I was stunned. I felt like someone had stabbed me in the heart. I barely noticed the audience giving us a standing ovation.

I returned to my seat. I couldn't even hear the next speaker being introduced. All I could hear were those words pounding in my ears. I felt so diminished, so unvalued. It felt like he thought I'd made a few copies, or collated a few packets. I had to sneak out of the room because I couldn't keep from crying.

I tried to tell myself that he knew I'd done more. He was present at the meetings I'd flown in for. He'd been Logistics Chair before. He knew all that I had done. Which made it hurt even more.

I was upset the rest of the day. His words had the opposite effect than he wanted. He hadn't thought about it before he opened his mouth.

You may have the opportunity to acknowledge your associates publicly. I implore you, beseech you, entreat you—think through your comments before you say them. Think: how would I like this honoree to feel after my comments?

Contrast that to a letter I received from Terry, the convention chair a few days later:

> Dear Rebecca:
>
> Thanks for being part of my all-star convention team! I couldn't have done it without you. Knowing you were in charge of logistics helped me focus on the general sessions. Your calm focus and follow through made it all possible.
>
> You've been with me for the long haul. Your discipline and invaluable experience came through over and over again.

I felt valued, acknowledged, and special. He had chosen words that were specific to me and what I had contributed. It was only six sentences, but the power of those six sentences helped ease the hurt from the president's blunder.

## *Words Can Make Us Feel Special*

How often have someone's few words made us feel special?

My friend, the late amazing speaker Rosita Perez, had a knack for saying the right thing. She was known in our professional organization as having close relationships with hundreds of her colleagues. Here's an excerpt from a note she sent to a friend:

> "When we left the hotel, we saw you briefly in the lobby. You were so quiet. I told Ray (her husband) 'Robert says so much to me, even without speaking. I just "hear" him in the silence.' That is a rare, rare, gift you have my friend. I guess that's why Ray and I think you are so special."

It was just a few words. Yet the power in Rosita's words. Robert felt valued and loved. She had touched his heart.

We all have that opportunity in our lives — to touch people's hearts. We can help a colleague feel better about the report that wasn't well received, or we can rub it in. We can "joke" when a friend is cheating on her diet, or we can acknowledge how difficult it is, and how we know she has the focus to stay on target. Our words can leave someone feeling empowered, or paralyzed.

Often it is hard to remember the specifics of positive, encouraging words. We can all remember someone in our life who had a major role in shaping who we are today through their loving, positive words. Perhaps it was a coach, teacher, relative, boss, or friend. Often we can't remember exactly what she or he said, but we know they made a difference in our life.

My friend Mary McGlynn is an example of this. She knows exactly what to say when I need some support. I can't quote specific words, yet I always feel better after having talked to her.

Without lecturing, Mary has a way of helping me see situations as learning opportunities. She doesn't negate the pain of a situation, but asks the right questions, and listens, really listens, to the answers.

Mary uses the power of her words to make everyone feel special. It's not in a sugary sweet, Pollyanna way, but in a sincere, genuine expression of her regard for that person. I've seen her do this not only with friends, but also with strangers she's barely met.

## *Healing Words*

The story of my high school friend, Dave Mulligan, is the most potent example of the power of words that I know.

At our 10 year reunion I watched him enter the room. In high school I'd harbored a not-so-subtle crush on him, even volunteering to keep score for the swim team so I could watch him compete in his Speedos.

Even ten years older, he looked like a Greek god—he was "Bay Watch" handsome, his blond curly hair setting off his striking blue eyes. He'd become a carpenter, so his athletic frame was filled out with strong muscles. I'm afraid I clung too long as he hugged me hello. He seemed to have everything going for him.

Five years later, all that changed. He took his first recreational parachute jump. The jump was going fine until he was 100 feet from the ground. The person guiding him from the ground gave him conflicting signals. Go right, no left. At about 50 feet Dave saw that he was going to run into either a row of cars, a trailer or a barbed wire fence. There was open space beneath him. It was his only chance. He had to land quickly.

As he'd been instructed to do in order to land quickly, he pulled his chute's strings hard. Too hard. His chute collapsed. He fell 40 feet straight down. It was the same as falling from a four story building.

Several vertebrae were crushed around his spinal cord. He was paralyzed from the waist down.

In the hospital after surgery, his doctors told him he'd never walk again. Although he had no feeling in the lower part of his body, he was determined to walk out of the hospital. When he kept insisting he was going to walk, the doctors insisted he see a psychiatrist to help him through his denial.

He was joined in his determination by his physical therapist, Helga. Every day she said, "Dave, wiggle your toes." Every day he tried and tried, yet couldn't. After each daily treatment, focusing on her words, he continued to try to wiggle his toes, determined to walk again. Helga didn't give up either, even though she knew what the doctors had said.

"You can do it; keep trying," she insisted. Everyday she encouraged and caringly hounded him with her words. He would struggle to wiggle his toes every waking hour. "This is now my full time job," he told himself, "toe wiggling. And I'm going to be the best toe wiggler there ever was."

After three weeks of trying for countless hours, his left big toe miraculously wiggled. Hallelujah! This meant there was a neural connection from his brain to his toe. Soon his other toes were wiggling. There was hope for him.

Bolstered by his success, he worked even harder to make his legs work. After only three months, he was amazingly able to walk with the aid of crutches. He was able to go from a paraplegic to ambulatory in an incredibly short amount of time. He now walks without crutches, and is not only happily married, but the father of a little girl.

Dave's determination, buoyed by Helga's persistence and words of encouragement, helped him change the outcome of his life. If he'd listened to his doctors words and had not been motivated continually by the simple power of Helga's words, he'd be in a wheelchair, and have a much different life.

When he shared this story, he told me,

> It seems very difficult to motivate our minds and especially our bodies to do things that are nearly impossible. The power of thought — for example, seeing someone running and wanting to do the same—was the most effective healing power for me, but also the hardest to stay focused on. However, the simple, constant 'chant' of 'wiggle your toes David' worked wonders to help continue that thought process and keep me focused.

We have opportunities every day to use our words to cut or to heal. Every time we open our mouth, We have a choice. You and I have the power to make others feel great — or horrible. With that power comes responsibility. We have the obligation to use that power in the best way possible for our fellow humans.

In my life's journey I'm learning to be vigilant in my awareness and sensitivity to not only the effect others' words have on me, but on the long-lasting effect my words have on others. It's true, "Words not only affect us temporarily—they change us."

Let's use the power of our words thoughtfully and positively to help prevent more pain on the planet and help heal the pain that's already here.

*Life's Lessons*

# Resources

Go to www.RebeccaMorgan.com to access a variety of useful resources.

## Management articles

We have over 200 pages of useful articles designed to help you manage your situations better.

## Managers Discussion Guide Program

This program enables you to make your staff meetings come alive in 20-30 minutes per month, with no prep by you!

## Books, MP3s and learning tools

High-quality tools to help you work more effectively.

## Blog

Read new ideas and stories to grow your key talent.

## Ezine

Subscribe to your free copy of *Insights and Information*, our periodic ezine full of tips and new ideas.

www.ingramcontent.com/pod-product-compliance
Lightning Source LLC
Chambersburg PA
CBHW072338300426
44109CB00042B/1751